INTRODUCING CANDLEMAKING

INTRODUCING
CANDLEMAKING

Paul Collins

Taplinger Publishing Company New York

First published in the United States in 1972 by
Taplinger Publishing Co Inc
New York, New York

Library of Congress Catalog Card Number: 72–563

ISBN   0–8008–4199–9

Contents

Introduction

In recent years there has been a revival of interest in candles and candle making. It is difficult to explain why candles continue to fascinate people in spite of the fact that they are no longer required as a basic source of illumination, so perhaps we should just accept that candles are useful, aesthetically pleasing and both easy and satisfying to make.

Candle making is a unique and exciting craft, in many ways similar to making pottery, but it does have two distinct advantages. The first is that no expensive specialized equipment is required, and the second is that the materials can be melted down and used again. This may be why the art of candle making has become not only a popular leisure time activity, but is taught in schools in both Europe and America, and practised in hospitals, where it is appreciated for its therapeutic value.

In the past, when candle making was an exclusively domestic art, everybody knew how to make them, what to make them from, and where to obtain the materials. Unfortunately this knowledge has been obscured by time and recently many people who have attempted to make candles have been discouraged by poor results due to lack of information and unsuitable materials. In this book I have attempted to describe the basic principles and processes of candle making, the sources of materials and to give some idea of the results which can be obtained. I hope that I have also succeeded in conveying some of the enjoyment of making beautiful candles.

1 Candlemaking techniques

There are three ways in which a candle can be made: the wax can be applied to the wick in layers, as in the *dipping and pouring* processes, or the wax can be cast around the wick in a solid mass with the aid of a candle mould. This last technique, *candle casting*, has been widely adopted by industry as the most efficient method of making candles in large quantities. From the domestic candle maker's point of view the choice of technique is not limited by the problems of mass production; the technique selected is a matter of personal preference.

In order to make use of the full potential of the various candle making techniques, it may help to understand how they evolved and what sort of materials were used with them originally.

In the past, candles were made from beeswax obtained from the honeycombs of bees, or tallow produced from the suet of beef, pork and mutton. Until the introduction of cotton into Europe in the Middle Ages, candle wicks were normally made from the peeled pith of rushes.

Tallow was not an ideal material for candle making as it tended to produce so much acrid smoke that it obscured the light. Beeswax, on the other hand, was ideal for making candles, it produced little smoke, gave more light and smelled of honey as it burned. Unfortunately beeswax has always been scarce and therefore expensive, whereas tallow has always been in plentiful supply and relatively cheap.

Tallow candles used to be called *tallow dips* as they were made by the *dipping* process. A large quantity of tallow was melted in a deep vat, the wicks were dipped into the molten tallow, removed, allowed to cool and the whole process repeated until the desired thickness had been built up on the wicks. A variation of this process was used to produce tapers: in this case the wick was pulled through a long shallow dish of molten tallow, and the tapers were cut up into the lengths required. This technique was developed after the advent of cotton had enabled wicks to be made of any length.

The technique which evolved for making candles in beeswax was characterized by the economical use of the wax. Instead of melting the wax in large quantities and dipping the wicks into the hot wax, the beeswax was melted in small containers and poured onto the suspended wick from a jug. Any surplus wax which dripped from the wick was collected in a dish for re-use. There was one disadvantage in candles made by this *pouring* process— they were lumpy and had an uneven surface. In the past this was remedied by rolling the lumpy candle between two pieces of hardwood or metal until the surface was acceptably smooth. Nowadays candles made by this technique are prized for the attractiveness of their sculptural qualities.

The technique of candle *casting* consists of using the melted wax to fill a mould in which the candle wick has been suspended. When the wax has set the finished candle can be removed from the mould with the wick firmly embedded in its centre. Before the invention of modern candle waxes such as paraffin wax and stearine, casting was limited to the use of tallow, as beeswax tended to adhere to the mould and could not be removed from the mould without re-melting. It is now possible to cast beeswax with the aid of modern silicone based release agents. These are used to coat the mould before filling with wax and act as a barrier which prevents the beeswax from adhering to the inside of the mould.

At first the idea of casting a candle mould may be rather intimidating, until one realizes that from the domestic candle maker's point of view a mould can be any con-

tainer which will tolerate the temperature of the hot wax and allow the candle to be removed after it has solidified. All sorts of containers which are to be found in any kitchen can be pressed into service as candle moulds—a cup for example will produce a chunky candle, a glass tumbler will produce a taller candle. A really exotic shape can be obtained by using a wine bottle, although the bottle does have to be broken in order to

11

remove the finished candle. On the other hand, it is possible for the more ambitious candle maker to design the shape of the candle and make the candle mould out of such familiar materials as cardboard or plaster. In industry the candle moulds are made from metal but excellent results can be obtained with much cheaper materials which can be easily used in the home.

The one advantage of casting is the variety of decorative effects possible. These methods of decorating candles are of very little interest to the large commercial candle manufacturers, but are of enormous interest to the domestic candle maker who derives satisfaction from creating something unique. Cast candles can be almost any shape. They can be striped in any colour, made to look like mosaic, or the wax can be marbled, painted or carved. In fact the decorative possibilities are only limited by the imagination and skill of the candle maker.

Although beeswax and tallow are still obtainable, most candles are now made from modern candle wax blends generally based on paraffin wax. But this does not affect the techniques of candle making; beautiful candles can be made from modern candle waxes both with and without the use of a mould. Each of the three techniques has its own characteristic appearance which is difficult to simulate by any other process. The *dipped* candle is characteristically cigar shaped; this is because the weight of the wax on the wick causes it to sag slightly. The *poured* candle has a very attractive natural sculptural appearance, and the cast candle is characterized by the richness and variety of the decorative effects possible. There is one further visual difference between candles made by the various processes and that is surface finish. The cast candle reproduces the finish of the interior of the mould. If the mould is polished and glossy the candle will also look polished and glossy. But in the case of candles made by the moulder's techniques of dipping and pouring, they acquire a natural satin like finish, rather similar to the bloom on a grape, which is extremely attractive.

2 How a candle works

A candle can be defined as a source of artificial light made by embedding a fibrous cotton wick in a solid block of wax. From this definition it can be seen that a candle consists of two components, the wick and the wax.

When the wick is lit, the flame radiates sufficient heat to melt a small pool of wax at the top of the candle. The liquid wax is then drawn up the wick by capillary action into the flame where it is vaporized and burnt (*figure 1*). It is not possible to burn wax unless it has first been super-heated into a vapour. The size of the flame is important as it should be related to the diameter of the candle. If the wick used is too thick, it will cause a large flame which generates so much heat that it prevents the formation of the bowl of molten fuel, by melting the outer edge or rim. This causes the molten wax to overflow and run down the side of the candle. On the other hand, if a wick which is too small is used, the small flame is not capable of genera-ting sufficient heat to form a proper reservoir of molten fuel, as the heat radiated will not reach the edge of the candle. This results in the flame burning a hole down the centre of the candle until it is so far down that it will go out through lack of oxygen (*figure 2*). It is therefore necessary to relate the wick size to the diameter of the candle. This need not be complicated, a thin wick should be used for candles with a diameter of 25 mm (1 in.) or less, a medium size wick should be used for candles of a 50 mm (2 in.) diameter, and a thick wick for 75 mm (3 in.) and over.

An additional function of the wick is to provide a venue

Figure 1

Figure 2

Figure 3

for the flame. This is a particularly complex function because the candle becomes shorter as it burns and the flame must follow the wax down. In other words both the wax and the wick must be consumed at the same rate. If this did not occur then as the level of the wax went down, the wick would become longer as more of it was exposed by the receding level of wax. This would result in a very large flame, as the extra length of wick would draw up more liquid wax, and this would inevitably result in a candle that burned down very rapidly. In the past this problem was solved by trimming the wick regularly, but now this is not necessary as modern candle wicks are made to be self consuming. This is achieved by braiding the cotton and saturating the wick in chemicals. The braiding causes the wick to bend slightly in the flame, bringing its tip into the hottest part of the flame (*figure 3*). The chemicals respond to the excess heat and reduce the wick to a very fine ash which is not capable of drawing up more liquid wax. In this way the exposed length of wick remains constant, and accompanies the level of wax as the candle burns down.

As the main purpose of the wax is to provide the fuel for the flame, the burning characteristics of the wax are extremely important. A good candle wax should produce a candle which burns steadily, lasts for a long time, produces very little smoke and gives a good quality light.

The rate at which a candle burns can be varied by using waxes which melt at different temperatures. A wax with a high melting point (the temperature at which it becomes liquid) will produce candles which last for a long time, whereas candles made from waxes with low melting points burn for a much shorter period.

Each different type of wax has its own special properties. For example, waxes with a low melting point tend to be comparatively soft and have good powers of adhesion. These characteristics are extremely useful when making candles by the dipping or pouring techniques. In these processes, the wax is built up on the wick in

14

layers, and it is essential that the individual layers adhere together. If the candle is made purely from low temperature wax, although the separate layers will adhere together, the candle will not burn for very long. But if another harder high temperature wax is added to the basic paraffin wax then the resulting blend will possess the desirable qualities of both waxes. The layers of wax will adhere together and the candle will burn at a much slower rate.

It is possible to make quite acceptable candles using nothing other than a general purpose medium temperature paraffin wax. But if really exceptional results are required, it is essential to use a blend of several waxes. The advantage of blending waxes is that all the desirable features can be combined into one candle wax.

Apart from its use as a fuel, candle wax also has other functions. It must be rigid enough to support the wick in a vertical position, it must be suitable for processing by one of the various candle making techniques, and it must look good.

Most paraffin waxes with a melting point within the range 52°C to 66°C (125°F to 150°F) are suitable for making candles. However there are differences in appearance, as in their natural state they vary from opaque to translucent white. The opaque waxes take dye particularly well and should be used if vivid colouring is required. The translucent waxes tend to darken colours until the candles are lit. When alight, the whole mass of the candle is illuminated from within as the light penetrates the translucent wax and is diffused throughout its entire mass.

3 Candlemaking equipment

In theory, all that is needed to make a candle is candle wick, wax, dye and a saucepan in which to melt the wax. In practice, better results can be obtained if a few refinements are added. For example, a thermometer enables the temperature of the wax to be controlled. Temperature control is essential when either pouring or dipping a candle as if the wax is too hot, not only will it not deposit, it will melt off wax that has already been deposited. In the case of casting, the temperature of the wax is just as important, although for a completely different reason. If the wax is too cool when it is poured in a mould, small air bubbles will be trapped between the surface of the mould and the wax, and will spoil the finished appearance of the candle. If on the other hand the wax is very much too hot, then it will distort considerably as it cools, spoiling the shape of the finished candle.

Although no expensive specialized equipment is necessary for making candles and all the essential equipment is to be found in any reasonably well-equipped kitchen, it may not be considered desirable to use the best hardware for candle making. It may be better to select the technique of candle making by a process of elimination, according to the hardware which is available for use.

Each of the three candle making techniques has a different requirement as far as equipment is concerned. There are however certain items which are required in each case, for example kitchen scales to measure the right proportion of waxes, in order to make a good candle wax blend, a small measuring spoon for measuring small quantities of dye and a thermometer to control the temperature.

The candle pouring process

The technique consists of suspending a wick over a container of melted wax and pouring hot wax from a jug so that it runs down the wick, cooling as it goes. Any surplus wax drips back into the saucepan and can be used again.

Equipment
1 Kitchen scales
2 Thermometer—a confectionery thermometer is ideal
3 A measuring spoon for the dye if it is in powder form
4 A saucepan in which to blend and melt the candle wax
5 A jug—small enough to dip into the saucepan

The candle dipping process

This technique consists of immersing the candle wick into molten wax, withdrawing it, allowing it to cool, and repeating the whole process until the desired thickness of wax has been built up on the wick.

The only disadvantage of the dipping process is that a deep vat is essential. This is because the depth of melted wax has to be slightly greater than the height of the candle to be made. The depth of the vat is important because the level of the wax will go down as it is deposited on the candle.

It is possible to transfer the melted wax from a saucepan to a deep metal jug, but it is not advisable to melt the wax in the jug as tall thin containers tend to be unstable.

Seamless aluminium containers, ideal for use as dipping vats and for melting wax are obtainable from many suppliers to the catering industry. A vat of seamless construction is recommended as all seams and joints are susceptible to leaking.

Equipment
1 Kitchen scales
2 Thermometer—a confectionery thermometer is ideal
3 A measuring spoon for use with the dye if it is in powder form

4   (a) A deep seamless metal vat—about 30 cm (12 in.) deep
    OR
    (b) A saucepan in which to melt the wax
    (c) A tall metal jug for dipping

The candle casting process
The casting technique consists of filling a mould, in which the wick has been suspended, with melted wax, allowing the wax to cool, and then removing the completed candle from the mould. Candle casting is slightly more complicated than the other techniques because it requires the use of a mould, but many commonplace articles can be used as candle moulds with excellent results, for example a cup, a glass tumbler, a wine bottle. On the other hand it is possible to construct a candle mould quite easily and a chapter has been devoted to describing how it can be done.

Equipment
1   Kitchen scales
2   Thermometer—a confectionery thermometer is ideal
3   A small measuring spoon for use with the dye if it is in powder form
4   A fine mesh metal tea strainer to filter the wax if it is dirty
5   A funnel—not essential but it does reduce the possibility of spillage when filling the moulds
6   A candle mould
7   Silicone release agent—not essential as long as the wax is hard enough to separate easily from the mould
8   A knitting needle or dowel rod from which to suspend the wick
9   A metal washer or weight
10 A saucepan

Apart from the equipment mentioned, all that is required in order to make candles are the candle making materials, the waxes, dyes and candle wick.

19

4 Candlemaking materials

Most modern candles are made from a blend of several ingredients. They are paraffin wax, stearic acid (stearine) and micro crystalline wax.

Paraffin wax is distilled from coal and oil shales and semi refined grades are used by most candle makers. The melting points of the suitable waxes range from 52°C to 60°C (125°F to 150°F), and any one may be selected from this range. Paraffin wax is a translucent shade of bluish white and is usually supplied in the form of large blocks.

For our purposes, stearic acid and stearine can be regarded as the same thing. Stearine is the chief ingredient of many animal and vegetable fats. The stearic acid is separated from the stearine by a steam process and is a hard white wax-like material, normally supplied in the form of flakes. The function of stearic acid is threefold—it makes the candle more opaque, it forms a crystalline framework within the candle wax, improves the casting and burning characteristics and reduces the amount of smoke produced by the candle flame. The amount of stearic acid which should be used in a candle may vary from about 5% to 30%. In general terms the quality of the candle improves in direct proportion to the amount of stearic acid used—the more stearic acid the better the candle.

Micro crystalline wax is a highly refined by-product of the coal and petroleum industries. It has a much higher melting point than paraffin wax, in the region of 85°C to 98°C (185°F to 210°F). It is white and generally supplied in the form of flakes. Its main characteristic is hardness. It deposits a hard skin on the surface of the candle which improves the appearance by giving it a shiny polished surface, and is hard enough to be resistant to minor damage. It also assists in ensuring a good release from the mould as it is too hard to adhere. Approximately 2% to 3% of micro crystalline wax should be used in order to produce a good quality candle.

A perfectly adequate simple candle can be made using nothing other than paraffin wax, but if a really superb candle is required, which will look marvellous, need little attention while burning and last for an exceptionally long time, then additives must be used.

As waxes from different suppliers tend to vary slightly —some are more opaque than others, some have a higher oil content, and some are characteristically harder than others—it is better to experiment with whatever waxes are available in order to develop the most suitable blend. They can all be used with equal success. It may be more convenient if material can be bought from a candle making company as then the best blends for those waxes are known. It is often possible to buy pre-mixed blends which already contain everything necessary to produce the best results. But if this is not possible then it is as well to know the principles by which modern waxes can be blended into high quality candle wax.

Candle wax consists basically of paraffin wax to which relatively small quantities of stearic acid and micro crystalline wax have been added. The exact proportion of the blend depends on the required burning characteristics and intended method of manufacture. If a long burning candle is required and it is intended to make it by the casting process, the basic paraffin wax selected should be hard, with a high melting point in the region of 60°C to 66°C (140°F to 150°F). The longevity will be further improved by the addition of a relatively large percentage of stearic acid, between 15% and 30%. A good surface finish resistant to abrasion and dust penetration can be obtained by adding 3% of micro crystalline wax, which will also ensure a good clean release from the mould as it is too hard to adhere.

When designing a blend for the dipping and pouring processes, the requirement is quite different as the wax is applied to the wick in layers and it is important to be certain that the wax is glutinous enough to make individual layers adhere together. This means that a softer paraffin wax is required with a melting point in the region of 52°C to 57°C (125°F to 135°F). The stearic acid is still required in the same proportions, 15% to 30%, if a long burning candle is required, but no micro crystalline wax should be used as it deposits at a faster rate than other waxes and therefore would cause the formation of hard substrates between the layers which could lead to delamination through poor adhesion.

If only soft waxes are available and a cast candle is required, then a silicone based release agent is necessary to facilitate removal from the mould. Silicone release agents form a barrier between the wax and the mould surface and prevent adhesion occurring. They are available in the form of semi-permanent coatings, which have to be baked on the mould, or a grease which has to be wiped on, or a liquid coating which can be sprayed on from an aerosol can. The most convenient one from the domestic candle maker's point of view is the aerosol dispenser.

Modern candle wicks are made from plaited or braided cotton which has been saturated in a solution of chemicals in order to make it burn down more or less at the same rate as the wax. For those enthusiasts who might like to make their own wicks the chemicals are potassium nitrate, borax, or ammonium chloride. After pickling the wick it is important to allow it to dry out completely, otherwise the water content will prevent the candle from burning properly.

Oil soluble dyes are essential for colouring wax. Care should be taken in the selection of dyes as crude dye with too much pigment will inhibit the burning of the candle. Some dyes are only soluble in a fatty acid, and require to be pre-mixed with stearine or stearic acid before being added to the paraffin wax.

22

No dye is completely colourfast in wax. If the same dye is used to colour both paint and wax then in paint it would have a colour fastness rating of 7, in wax it would have a rating of 3.

Although candles are now not normally made from beeswax and tallow, some people may enjoy experimenting with these ancient materials.

Beeswax is the wax from the honeycomb of the bee. It is obtained by melting the honeycomb in hot water, straining it and allowing it to cool. At this stage it is a brownish yellow colour. If it is intended for use in candles it is then bleached to a yellowish white colour.

Tallow is a hard fat and may be of animal or vegetable origin. It can be produced from the rendered suet of animals or from the fruits of certain trees such as the bay tree, the Japanese sumach tree or the Chinese tallow tree. The fruits are steamed in a perforated kettle and the fat which is melted constitutes vegetable tallow. The main ingredients of tallow are stearine, palmetin and olein.

5 The dipping process

As the name implies, the technique of candle dipping consists of literally dipping the wick into a deep vat of molten wax (*figure 6*). After waiting a few seconds for the wax to coat the wick, it is removed from the vat and the wax allowed to cool. The process of dipping and cooling is then repeated until the desired thickness of wax has been built up on the wick.

As far as the domestic candle maker is concerned, there are two drawbacks to the dipping process. The first is that a deep vat must be used. It is essential that the depth of melted wax is slightly greater than the height of the candle being made, otherwise the wax would not completely cover the candle each time it was dipped. An additional reason for the extra depth of wax is that its level goes down as the wax is deposited on the candle. The second drawback is that there must be sufficient wax to fill the vat, even a small vat about 300 mm (12 in.) deep and 200 mm (8 in.) in diameter will require about 7 kg (15 lb) of wax to fill it.

The most suitable type of vat for use with this technique is of seamless steel or aluminium. If a seamless vat is used then it can also be utilized to melt the wax. It is important to remember that wax should never be melted in any sort of container which has seams, as a leak would inevitably result in liquid wax dripping directly on to the heat source, and this could be dangerous. Suitable metal vats of seamless construction are obtainable in a variety of sizes from many suppliers to the catering industry.

Figure 6 Making a candle by the dipping process

There is an alternative to the use of a special seamless vat and that is to use a saucepan to melt the wax, and a tall enamel jug or similar metal container as a dipping vat. There is one disadvantage when using such domestic utensils for candle making and that is the difficulty of removing the wax once it has set. Most tall metal domestic jugs are made so that they are wider at the bottom than at the top. This is done to improve their stability, but when used as a dipping vat, this shape means that it will be impossible to remove the wax in solid form. The narrow neck at the top forms an obstruction or undercut which prevents the withdrawal of the solid wax. As jugs of this type are usually fabricated from sheet metal, and have seams, it is not advisable to re-melt the wax by heating the jug as all seams are subject to leaking. So unless it is possible to find a tall metal utensil which is wider at the top than at the bottom, with no undercuts to prevent the removal of the solid wax, the answer is to decant the wax from the jug back into the saucepan immediately after dipping while the wax is still in liquid form.

The dipping process of candle making was originally limited to the use of tallow. This was not because beeswax candles could not be manufactured by this process, but because beeswax was always in short supply whereas tallow was generally in abundance. As common tallow tends to smell offensively and produce a great deal of acrid smoke it is unlikely that the domestic candle maker will choose to use this material, although it is still obtainable. It is more likely that a candle wax blend based on paraffin wax will be selected.

It is possible to make perfectly adequate candles by the dipping process using paraffin wax to which nothing has been added. If an unblended paraffin wax is to be used, it is important to select one with the right characteristics. It should have a melting point of between 52°C and 54°C (125°F and 130°F); in certain cases if the wax has high oil content the range may be extended to 54°C to 57°C (130°F to 135°F). The wax should be semi-refined and tending towards opacity rather than translucency. This is because an opaque wax will disguise any slight delamination that occurs. As the wax is applied in thin even layers, if the paraffin wax is too translucent, it is sometimes possible to see light patches where slight delamination has occurred between the separate layers of wax.

Delamination is no problem when a candle wax blend is used as adhesive qualities can be incorporated into the blend. As waxes from different suppliers tend to vary slightly it is difficult to be precise about the exact proportions of a blend—it is better to experiment until the best proportions are discovered. A good starting point would be to obtain a semi refined paraffin wax of the opaque variety with a melting point in the region of 54°C (130°F). To this 20% of stearic acid, a white wax like substance, should be added. If the candle maker likes the smell of honey then a little, say 5%, of beeswax can be added. This will also improve the qualities of adhesion of the wax. Micro crystalline wax should be omitted altogether as it tends to deposit at a faster rate than other waxes and may prevent adhesion from occurring naturally.

Break the paraffin wax into pieces of a convenient size, weigh out the required quantity and place in the vat. Add to it the right quantity of stearic acid or stearine, and the beeswax if required. The dye can either be added now or later. If the candle is made entirely from coloured wax the colouring will not be as vivid as it would be if the candle is made in white wax and the colour applied in the last layer. If a really startling colour is required, then do not add the dye to the wax in the vat, until just before the final dipping operation.

Place the vat on the cooker and heat gently until all the contents have melted and blended together. When this occurs, allow the blend to cool to about 49°C (120°F) before attempting to dip. It is advisable to experiment with various temperatures to find the one which suits the blend best.

Apart from finding the best temperature at which to dip, the secret of a good dipping technique lies in a smooth action. The candle should be submerged in the wax and withdrawn as smoothly as possible so that the wax deposits an even layer with no drips or surface imperfection.

6 Making wax tapers

Wax tapers are made by a variation of the dipping process. The candle wax is placed in a shallow tray or trough which is then heated until the wax has melted. The wick is then drawn slowly through the trough so that it is coated with a generous layer of wax (*figure 4*).

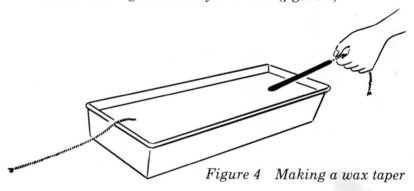

Figure 4   Making a wax taper

When making tapers it is important that the wax should not be too hot or it will only deposit a very thin coating. In general terms the cooler the wax, the thicker the layer deposited on the wick. A temperature in the region of 52°C (125°F) should be found satisfactory for most candle waxes.

It is possible to produce tapers in very long lengths by placing the bobbin of wick at one end of the trough, and connecting the lower end of the wick to a large diameter roller situated at the opposite end of the trough. When the roller is slowly rotated, the wick is dragged through

Figure 5a

28

the molten wax and coiled around the drum of the roller. All that is subsequently required is to cut the individual tapers to the required length.

If a particularly thick taper is required, it may be dipped more than once, but in this case a flexible softer wax, preferably containing about 10% of beeswax should be used.

A thin candle wick is usually used for making tapers, and a hard wax with a melting point in the region of 60°C to 66°C (140°F to 150°F) will ensure that the taper burns for as long as possible.

Wax tapers can be used singly, or twisted together to make larger multiwick candles. If the tapers are twisted together along their entire length, the result is more reminiscent of a pitch torch than a candle because the flame produced is so large. The only disadvantage is that the taper torch does not last long.

Multibranch tapers can be made by twisting or plaiting together the bottom few inches of a number of tapers and bending the branches (*figure 5a and b*). If a hard wax was used to make the tapers, it may be necessary to warm them before attempting to bend or plait them. Tapers can be readily softened by dipping them into a jug or saucepan of warm water at a temperature in the region of 38°C (100°F).

An interesting coiled taper candle can be made by coiling the taper around a wooden plug, allowing a few inches of taper to project upwards to carry the flame (*figure 5c*). As the taper burns down, the coil is unwound to maintain the flame in the desired position. In the past such tapers were burned in front of a circular reflector which projected the light where it was required.

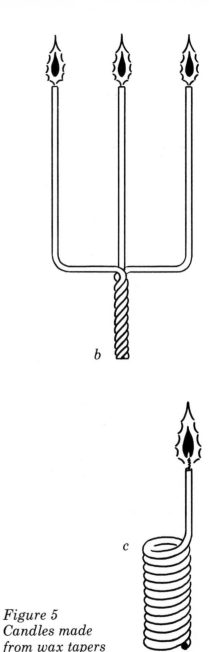

Figure 5
Candles made
from wax tapers

29

7 Making branch candles by the dipping process

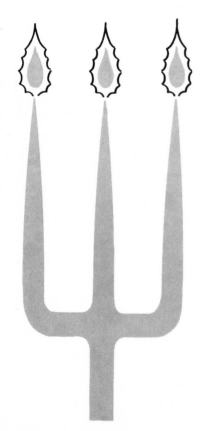

Figure 7 A branch candle made by the dipping process

A branch candle made by the dipping process differs from one made by the pouring process in that the dipped branch candle has a single stem which divides to become the individual branches, whereas the poured branch candle has branches which rise straight up from the base of the candle.

Dipped branch candles are made by repeatedly dipping a group of candle wicks into a vat of molten wax instead of a single wick as described in the previous chapter. Each dipping operation deposits a coating of wax on the wicks and is repeated until a sufficient thickness of wax is obtained.

The grouping of the wicks is achieved with the aid of a dipping frame. The dipping frame does not have to be elaborate, for most purposes a short length of dowel rod is quite adequate. Only in the case of the more complicated wick arrangements is it necessary to fabricate several pieces of wood together as illustrated.

As an example of making a branch candle by the dipping process, let us consider making a candle with three branches (*figure 7*). The size of the branch candle will be limited by the size of the dipping vat. This example is based on the use of a vat 305 mm (12 in.) tall and 205 mm (8 in.) in diameter.

Equipment

A metal vat of seamless construction in which to melt the

wax and dip the wicks, and a confectionery thermometer

Materials
Sufficient candle wax to fill the vat. A vat 305 mm (12 in.)
deep and 205 mm (8 in.) in diameter will require about
7 kg (16 lb) of candle wax to fill it
1015 mm (40 in.) of candle wick
205 mm (8 in.) of sewing cotton
A short length of 6 mm ($\frac{1}{4}$ in.) dowel rod, approximately
180 mm (7 in.) will be needed for making a three branch
candle
1 dessert spoonful of oil soluble dye.

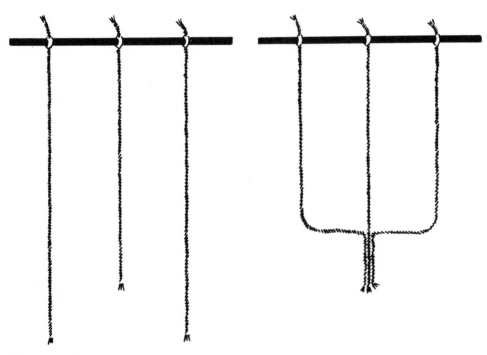

Figure 8   *Figure 9*

To make the candle

Place the selected candle wax in the seamless metal vat, add the oil soluble dye and heat gently. When all the wax has melted, switch off the heat and allow the molten wax to cool.

Cut the candle wick into three pieces, two of which should be about 75 mm (3 in.) longer than the other. Tie

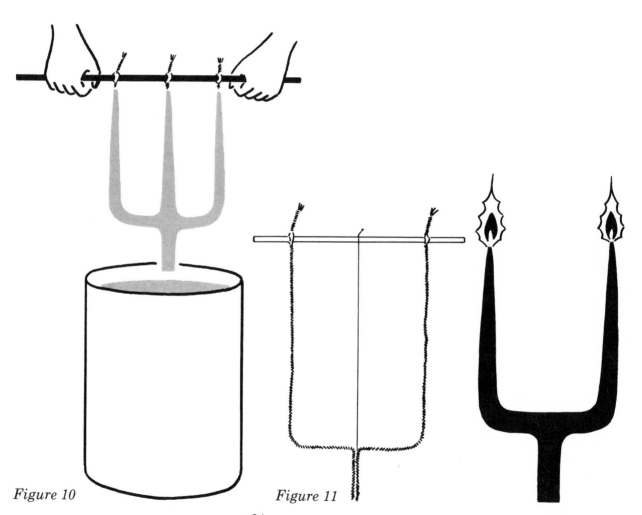

Figure 10

Figure 11

one end of the short length of wick to the centre of the wooden dowel rod, allowing the other end to hang free. Then tie the two longer wicks on either side of the shorter wick, spacing them about 105 mm (4 in.) apart (*figure 8*). Finally bind the bottom 50 mm (2 in.) of all the wicks together with cotton and the wick configuration is ready for dipping (*figure 9*). If much distortion occurs in the shape while dipping, a weight should be tied to the bottom of the central stem—a small metal nut should serve the purpose admirably.

Almost any number of branches can be incorporated into a branch candle, and various other wick configurations are shown in *figures 11 and 12*.

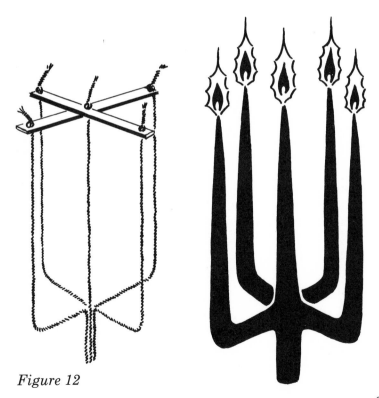

Figure 12

8 The pouring process

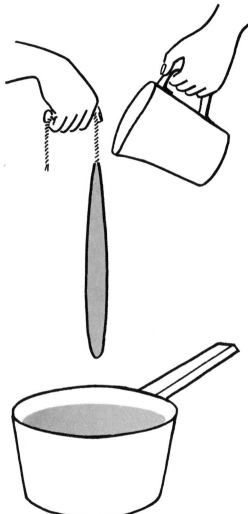

Figure 13   *Making a candle by the pouring process*

The technique of candle pouring consists of literally pouring molten wax from a jug onto a suspended candle wick (*figure 13*), so that the wax runs down the wick becoming solid as it descends. Any wax which has not set by the time it reaches the bottom of the wick drips into a dish and is eventually re-melted and used again. The process of pouring is repeated continually until the desired thickness of wax is built up on the wick.

This technique was originally developed for use with beeswax, and is an excellent solution to the problem of making a little wax go a long way. Beeswax was rarely available in large quantities so it was necessary to develop a technique which did not depend on having a large vat full of molten wax as in candle dipping.

Although it is still possible to obtain beeswax, it is expensive and it is unlikely that this material will be selected for candle making, but if it is used, the technique of candle making remains exactly the same. Instead of beeswax the domestic candle maker is likely to want to use a paraffin wax blend. It is possible to make candles by the pouring process using only paraffin wax. If this is the objective then an opaque semi refined paraffin wax with a melting temperature of 52°C to 54°C (125°F to 130°F) is required. Such a wax will produce quite acceptable results, but for the best results a blend should be used consisting of paraffin wax with a melting point of 52°C to 54°C (125°F to 130°F) with between 20% and 30% of stearic acid. Such a blend will produce a poured candle of excellent quality which will burn well, last well and give

36

very good light. The low temperature paraffin wax is necessary to ensure that the separate layers of candle wax bond together into a cohesive whole. No micro crystalline wax should be used as it deposits at a faster rate than other waxes and is too hard to adhere to the layer of wax below it.

Weigh the paraffin wax, break it into manageable pieces and place in a saucepan. Work out the right percentage of stearic acid, measure it out and add to the paraffin wax in the saucepan. Measure out the oil soluble dye; it is advisable to be careful with the dye as very little is required to colour one candle. Half a level teaspoonful is more than enough to colour two or three large candles. Place the saucepan on the cooker and heat it gently until the wax has melted.

When all the wax has melted, and the dye has dissolved, remove the saucepan from the heat source and allow the wax to cool slightly. This is important as if the wax is poured too hot, it will not deposit but just run down the wick and drip off without solidifying at all. If there is already wax on the wick and more wax is applied at too high a temperature, then the wax which has already been deposited will be melted off, so it is important to allow the wax to cool before pouring. As the characteristics of different waxes vary considerably, it is difficult to be precise about the best temperature at which to pour. It is better to experiment with whatever wax has been obtained with a view to establishing the most suitable temperature. In general terms, allow the wax to cool to about 5° under its melting point before pouring.

While the wax is cooling, the candle wick can be prepared. When cutting it to the desired length, a few centimetres (inches) extra should be allowed as it will either have to be held or suspended in some other way over the saucepan.

When the wick is ready and the wax has cooled sufficiently, take a jug, dip it into the molten wax and pour it so that it runs down the wick. Some of it will drip back into the saucepan. Allow the wax on the wick to cool completely, and then pour on more wax. Repeat the whole process of pouring and allowing to cool until the desired thickness of wax has been built up on the wick.

Although poured candles are characterized by their knobbly surface, it is possible to minimize or emphasize this feature of their appearance. If a smoother shape is preferred, then as the wax is poured the wick should be rotated slowly so that the wax coating is as evenly distributed as possible. If a really rough surface is required then pour the wax erratically, making no effort to allow it to coat the candle evenly. The lumpiness can be exaggerated further by allowing the wax to cool in the saucepan, almost to the point of setting.

There is a problem with pouring waxes at too low a temperature and that is that it will not bond to the surface below. The result of this lack of adhesion is known as delamination. Delamination should not occur when the wax is poured normally, only if it is very cool when poured. This can often be cured by adding a little beeswax —about 5% to the blend—or just raising the temperature at which the wax is poured by about 10°.

The final coating of the candle should be poured as evenly as possible. If this is done carefully the surface will acquire a bloom which gives it a satin like finish which is most attractive.

Although it is not possible to accurately control the shape of a poured candle, the shape can be influenced by applying more wax over particular areas of the candle. In this way the shape can be varied by making some parts of the candle thicker than others.

9 Making branch candles by the 'pouring' process

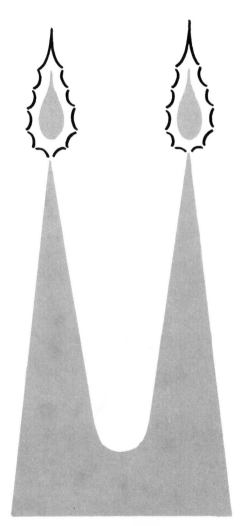

Branch candles can be made by both the pouring and the dipping processes, but each manufacturing technique produces characteristically different results in appearance. The dipped branch candle has a single central stem which abruptly divides into separate branches whereas the poured branch candle has separate branches which rise straight up from the base of the candle.

Poured branch candles are made by pouring the hot wax over a group of candle wicks instead of over a single candle wick as described in the previous chapter. The pouring technique remains the same, but before the wax is added, the wicks must be assembled together so that they will all become part of the same candle after pouring. The assembly of the wicks is achieved with the aid of a simple frame, or to be more accurate two identical simple frames, one at the top of the wicks and one at the bottom.

The function of the frames is to hold the wicks in position while the candle is being poured, but the lower frame also becomes part of the candle as it will be firmly embedded inside the wax when the candle is finished.

The frames need not be elaborate, in fact in most cases a short length of dowel rod or even a pencil will do. Only for complicated wick arrangements is it necessary to go to the length of using bent wire for the frames.

As an example of pouring a branch candle let us consider making a simple two branch candle (*figure 14*).

Figure 14 A branch candle made by the pouring process

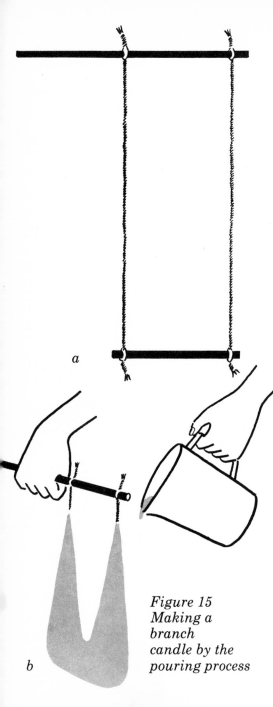

a

b

*Figure 15
Making a
branch
candle by the
pouring process*

Equipment
A small saucepan in which to melt the wax
A dish to catch any excess which drips off during the
pouring process
A small jug
A confectionery thermometer

Materials
610 mm (2 ft) of candle wick
254 mm (10 in.) of 6 mm ($\frac{1}{4}$ in.) dowel rod
1 kg (3 lb) of candle wax
A level teaspoonful of oil soluble dye

To make the branch candle
Place whichever candle wax is to be used in a saucepan,
add the oil soluble dye, heat it gently, and stir until all the
wax has melted and the dye dissolved, then remove the
saucepan from the heat source and allow it to cool.

Cut both the dowel rod and the candle wick in half, and
tie the wicks to the dowel as illustrated (*figure 15a*)
making sure that they are spaced about 100 mm (4 in.)
apart.

When the temperature of the wax in the saucepan has
dropped to about 71°C (160°F), some of it can be decanted
into the jug and the pouring process can be started
(*figure 15b*). Although the saucepan can be placed under
the wicks to catch any excess wax that drips off, it is
better to use a separate dish to catch the drips as otherwise they would result in a particularly lumpy candle.
Each layer of wax shall be allowed to cool for a while
before the next layer is poured.

When the pouring operation is finished, and the bottom
dowel is deeply embedded in the wax, all that remains to
be done is to cut the wicks at the top leaving about 12 mm
($\frac{1}{2}$ in.) projecting from the top of the candles, and trim the
bottom of the candle flat with a sharp knife.

Almost any number of wicks can be incorporated into
a poured branch candle, but they should be at least
75 mm (3 in.) apart. If they are closer, then the close

proximity of the flames in the finished candle, will cause it to burn unevenly. Other wick configurations are shown in *figures 16 and 17*.

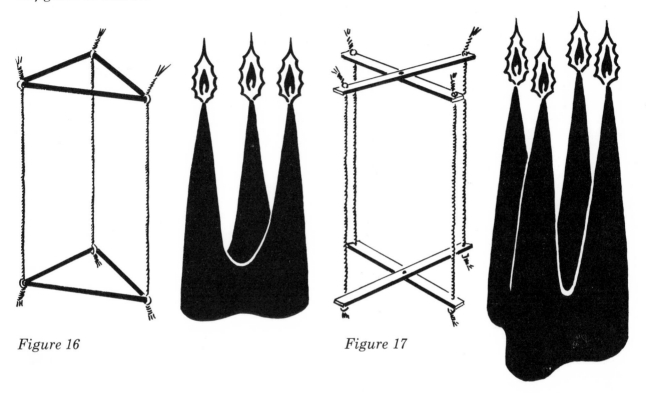

Figure 16

Figure 17

41

10 Rolling a candle

The technique of candle rolling is particularly suitable for very young children as it does not involve the use of molten wax. It simply consists of rolling a sheet of wax around the candle wick (*figure 18*).

Many different types of wax are obtainable in sheet form, but the most common are beeswax and paraffin wax.

Sheet beeswax is produced with a honeycomb texture and is used to provide a central core in beehives. In order to make one pound of beeswax, bees consume nearly seven pounds of honey and pollen, so beekeepers provide a honeycomb core so that the bees can get down to the real work of making the honey and building up the honeycomb cells for winter storage and larvae.

Sheet paraffin wax is made in many thicknesses and is used for making shell moulds in industry. Paraffin wax sheets 2 mm ($\frac{1}{16}$ in.) to 3 mm ($\frac{1}{8}$ in.) thick are most suitable for candle making.

To make the candle from sheet beeswax
With a pair of scissors, cut the sheet into a rectangle of the desired size. The length of the sheet will determine the diameter of the candle and the width should be cut to about a half inch less than the length of the wick.

To obtain a conical candle top, cut the top of the sheet at an angle as illustrated (*figure 19*).

Then press the wick into the longer of the two short sides, and simply roll up the wax so that the wick is enclosed in the middle of the roll (*figure 20*).

Figure 18
A rolled candle

To make the candle from sheet paraffin wax
As sheet paraffin wax tends to be harder and more difficult to bend, it may be necessary to warm the sheet first. This can be done over a radiator, or in a low temperature domestic oven, or even in hot water (about 41°C (105°F)) providing the wick is first soaked in molten wax to prevent it from absorbing water from the wet sheet of wax. Otherwise the rolling technique is exactly the same as for a beeswax sheet.

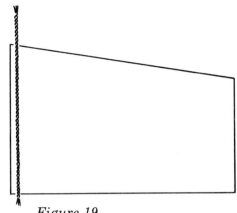

Figure 19

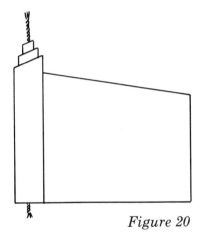

Figure 20

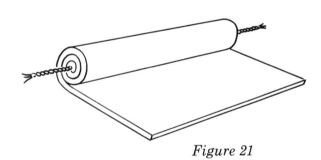

Figure 21

Casting a sheet of wax
If sheet wax is not readily available, wax can be cast into shallow trays such as baking tins, or in specially made box moulds as illustrated (*figure 24*). In both cases a silicone release agent should be used to prevent the wax

43

from adhering to the mould, and the molten wax should not be more than 82°C (180°F) when it is poured into the mould.

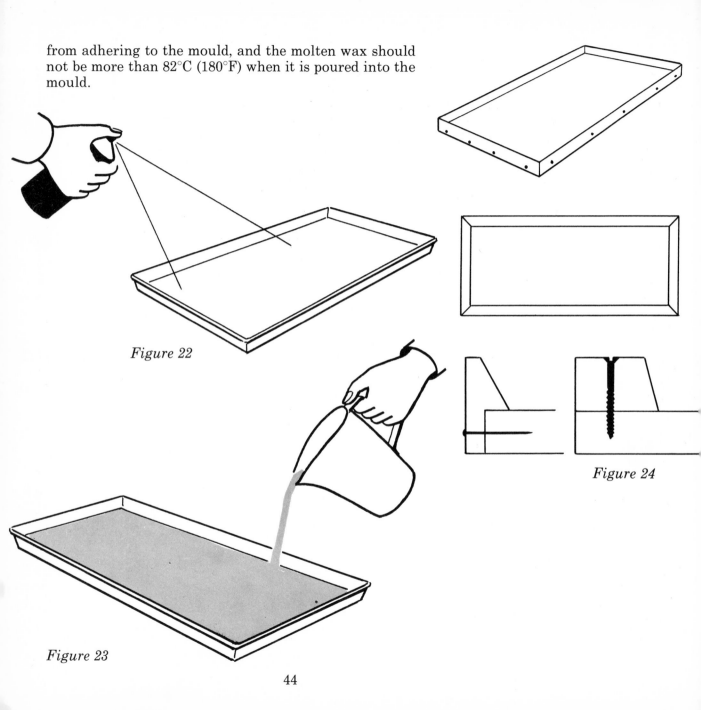

Figure 22

Figure 23

Figure 24

11 The casting process

The technique of candle casting consists of suspending a wick in a mould and then filling the cavity of the mould with molten wax (*figure 25*). When the wax has cooled and set, the finished candle can be removed from the mould and will be an exact replica of the inside shape of the mould.

Since the invention of the candle mould in the fifteenth century, casting has become the most popular technique for making candles. This is largely because it was found to be particularly suitable for producing candles in large quantities. In fact modern candle making machines contain many hundreds of individual moulds and are often capable of producing several thousand finished candles each hour.

The candle making machine as we now know it was invented in the middle of the nineteenth century, and surprisingly few improvements have been made since they were first introduced. The principle on which they work is very simple. Each mould consists of a tapered metal tube, blocked at the bottom with a metal plug, which can be moved in an upward direction. Each mould has its own bobbin of wick fitted in the base of the machine with the wick running up through the centre of the mould (*figure 26*). After the mould has been filled, and the wax has set, the plugs are moved upwards so that they literally push the finished candles out of the moulds. The plugs are then returned to their original position at the bottom and the moulds are then ready to be refilled.

From the domestic candle maker's point of view,

Figure 25   Making a candle by the casting process

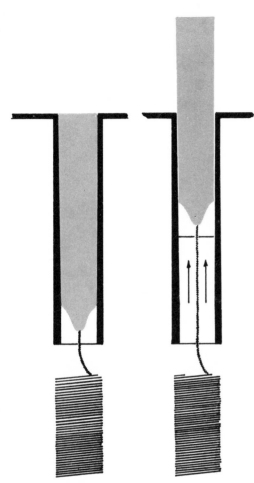

Figure 26

casting as a technique has three appreciable advantages. The first is the variety of shapes which can be obtained; almost any container which will hold hot wax without leaking, can be used as a candle mould. When choosing a suitable mould it is important to bear in mind that if it is not possible to remove the finished candle from the mould, the mould will have to be broken in order to extract the candle. Therefore the container should either have no undercuts or it should be disposable. It is also possible to design a candle and make a mould to reproduce the exact shape required. This need not be an expensive operation as adequate candle moulds can be made from such cheap materials as cardboard and plaster of paris.

A second advantage with casting is the lack of labour involved. Once the mould is filled, little remains to be done but to wait until the wax has set, and the candle can be removed from the mould.

The third advantage is the variety of visual effects which can be obtained with 'in mould' decorative techniques. These include stripes, marbling and mosaic effects. The various methods of 'in mould' decoration are described in Chapter 23.

A hard wax is required for casting as it is less likely to adhere to the mould. As hardness is synonymous with a high melting point, a wax which melts in the region of 60°C to 68°C (140°F to 155°F) is required.

The temperature for filling a mould should not be lower than 80°C (175°F) and not higher than 88°C (190°F).

Before filling the mould, the wick must be suspended. Tie one end of the wick to a wire or hairpin, anything will do that is wide enough to span the top of the mould. Weight the other end of the wick with a small metal nut or washer, and place the wire across the top of the mould so that the wick hangs down in the centre of the mould.

When the mould is full, allow it to cool slowly, do not attempt to accelerate the cooling process by putting the mould in a refrigerator as this may cause stress cracking and cavities within the candle.

After an hour or so, when the wax has started to set,

poke a stick or knitting needle down into the candle near the wick. This will relieve the vacuum which sometimes occurs in the middle of large candles. As the wax cools it shrinks, so add a little more wax every hour or so just to keep the top more or less level.

When the candle has completely set, it should be possible to lift it out of the mould without any trouble. If the candle does tend to bind in the mould, put it in the refrigerator for half an hour. This can be done without any adverse effects as long as the wax is solid, and will cause the wax to contract slightly enabling the candle to be withdrawn.

If the wax has really adhered to the mould, and resists all attempts at removal, it is likely that the wax is too soft for casting without the aid of a release agent. The only way to remove the wax is to melt it out. This should be done by placing the mould upside down in a saucepan or dish and heating it in an oven until the wax runs out. The mould should then be wiped clean with a paper tissue, and a silicone release agent used to prevent the same problem occurring again.

12 Candle moulds

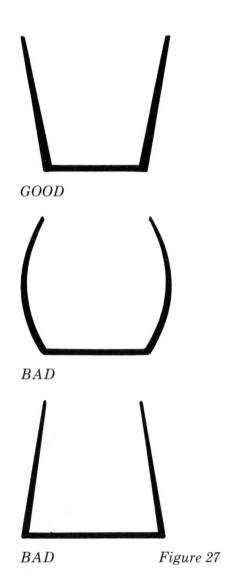

GOOD

BAD

BAD   *Figure 27*

Candle moulds fall into two distinct categories—the first consists of commonplace domestic articles which can be used as candle moulds, and the second of those moulds made specifically for the purpose of candle making.

The variety of domestic articles which can be used as candle moulds is enormous and includes such things as cups, glass tumblers, mugs, jugs and bottles. In fact almost any article made from pottery, glass or metal can be used and will give excellent results. Plastic articles are best avoided as some types of plastic collapse and disintegrate when filled with hot wax.

When selecting a domestic container for use as a candle mould it is important to check that there are no undercuts. In other words, it must be possible to remove the candle without destroying the mould (*figure 27*). For example, although it is possible to pour molten wax into a container with a narrow neck, it is not possible to withdraw the candle after the wax has set. Unless the mould is considered expendable, as in the case of a bottle which can be broken in order to remove the candle, the mould should be slightly wider at the top than at the bottom so that there are no obstructions to removing the candle.

Any container made from pottery and glazed inside can be used as a candle mould providing there are no undercuts. The glaze is important because wax will stick to unglazed pottery and it will be impossible to remove the finished candle.

Glass is a particularly suitable material for candle moulds as the candle can be seen while it is being made. It is however necessary to warm the glass before filling, as the abrupt change of temperature may cause the glass to crack.

Glass tumblers make excellent candle moulds, they are usually of exactly the right shape to allow withdrawal of the finished candle, and the smooth surface of the glass gives the candle a polished finish.

A wine bottle on the other hand, gives a very interesting shape but has to be broken in order to extract the candle. This can be done safely if the bottle containing the finished candle is placed in a plastic bag, the bottle broken and the candle removed from the bag leaving the broken glass inside. In this way the handling of broken glass can be avoided.

If a sufficiently attractive glass container is used as a mould, for example a wine glass, the candle can be left in the glass and the glass used as a decorative candle stick.

Tin cans come in many different shapes and sizes and produce very good results when used as candle moulds. It may be necessary however to cut off the top rim or seam of the tins as this might constitute an undercut and could prevent the removal of the finished candle. Wax should not be melted in a tin as the heat could melt the solder and the wax leak onto the heat source. A saucepan or similar seamless container should be used as a vat; a tin is only suitable for use as a mould.

There are many other metal articles in common use which can be used as candle moulds such as enamel mugs, stainless steel jugs, and flower holders—in fact any metal container which will allow the candle to be removed after it has been set.

In the candle making industry, candle moulds are usually made from high grade tin. Sometimes other metals are used such as aluminium, steel, lead alloy and bronze. But it is not necessary for the domestic candle maker to go to the expense of having professional metal candle moulds made, for there are several ways of making candle moulds at very low cost.

49

There are two extremely cheap materials which can be used to make candle moulds: fine grain cardboard and plaster of paris. The cardboard is useful for making one piece sheet moulds of such shapes as cones, pyramids and cubes. The plaster is more useful for more complex two piece moulds and is capable of reproducing compound shapes such as spheres, abstract forms and even figurines. It is essential that candle moulds made from both of these materials are sealed with good quality heat resistant polyurethane paint, as otherwise the wax may adhere to the porous surfaces of the moulds. Detailed information on the subject of making moulds in cardboard and plaster is given in the chapters on making conical and spherical candles.

Tin plate is also relatively cheap, and is available in thin metal sheets which can be fabricated into candle moulds, using similar techniques to those used for cardboard. The only difference is that the seams should be soldered, preferably with a high temperature solder, and must be turned outwards so that the seams do not obstruct the removal of the candle from the mould. The only problem with tin plate candle moulds is that they are susceptible to denting. If, however, they are treated with respect, they will give excellent service.

Excellent candle moulds can be constructed from metal pipes. Any metal pipe can be used as long as it is of seamless construction and smooth on the inside. A plug is required both to give shape to the end of the candle and to serve as an ejector if the candle proves difficult to remove from the mould (*figure 28*). The plug should be turned from a similar metal to that of the pipe in order to minimize the possibility of binding due to different coefficients of expansion.

Glass is particularly suitable for making candle moulds as it is extremely well finished and allows the candle to be seen while it is being made. Glass tubes are available in many sizes and can be used for making moulds as long as they are not plugged in the same way as metal tubes (*figure 29*). This is because a metal plug

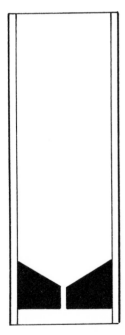

Figure 28   Candle mould constructed from metal tube and turned metal plug

would expand with the heat and crack the glass. A rubber bung can be used, but the best answer is a silicone rubber or flexible polyurethane cap. In both cases the manufacturing technique is the same. Take the glass tube which is to be used, and block one end with plasticine (*figure 30a*). Add more plasticine, and use it to model the shape required for the top of the candle. Press a thin knitting needle into the plasticine, and leave it there to form a hole for the wick in the cap. Then construct a cardboard container with an internal diameter about 12 mm ($\frac{1}{2}$ in.) bigger than the external diameter of the glass tube. Cut a hole the size of the glass tube in the bottom of this container and place it over the top of the glass mould as illustrated (*figure 30b*), and fill with cold cure silicone rubber or polyurethane elastomer. When this has set (the technical term is *cured*), the cardboard surround can be removed and the glass tube and plasticine model withdrawn, leaving a flexible cap which will fit exactly on the end of the glass tube and give the top of the candle the required shape (*figure 30c*).

Figure 29   Candle mould made from glass tube and rubber bung

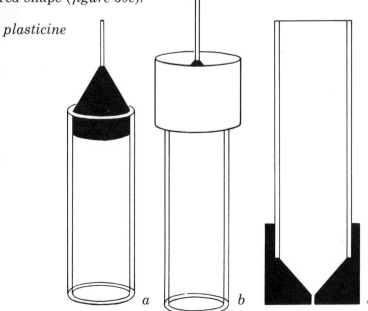

plasticine

cardboard cylinder

a   *b*   *c*

Figure 30   Making a polyurethane or silicone rubber cap for a glass tube candle mould

51

13 Making a candle in a wine glass

Figure 31

Materials
227 g (½ lb) of candle wax
100 mm (4 in.) of candle wick
¼ of a level teaspoonful of oil soluble dye

Equipment
A small saucepan with a pouring lip, in which to melt the wax
The wax will not damage the saucepan, and any wax left after making the candle can be lifted out after it has cooled
A confectionery thermometer is useful, but not absolutely essential
A metal pouring funnel will reduce the possibility of spillage, but is not essential
A short length of stiff wire about an inch longer than the width of the wine glass. A hairpin, nail or even a pencil will do.
A metal weight (a small nut or washer will do)
An attractive wine glass

To make the candle
Break the paraffin wax into small pieces, place them in the saucepan and add the oil soluble dye. Heat the saucepan gently and make sure that all the dye has dissolved by stirring the wax a few times. When all the wax has melted remove the saucepan from the cooker and allow it to cool slightly.

Warm the wine glass in an oven or over a gas jet. Do not dip it in hot water as hot wax and water do not mix and will splutter and spit unpleasantly.

Take the candle wick and tie one end of it to the centre of the metal rod, then tie the metal weight to the other end of the wick (*figure 32a*). Now place the metal rod across the rim of the glass so that the wick hangs down as illustrated (*figure 32b*).

All that now remains to be done is to pour the wax into the wine glass. The wax should be poured at about 82°C (180°F), but if there is no thermometer, look carefully at the hot wax and if there is a little smoke rising from it, the temperature is too high and it should be allowed to cool for a little.

After the wax has set, untie the metal rod and cut the exposed wick so that only about 12 mm ($\frac{1}{2}$ in.) is left visible. Do not attempt to remove the candle from the glass. Leave it there and use the glass as an attractive candle stick.

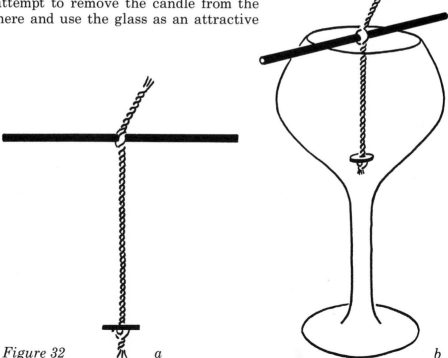

Figure 32   *a*   *b*

14 Making a candle in a cup

Materials
227 g ($\frac{1}{2}$ lb) of paraffin wax with a melting point of 60°C to 63°C (140°F to 145°F)
100 mm (4 in.) of candle wick
$\frac{1}{4}$ of a level teaspoonful of oil soluble dye

Equipment
A small saucepan, preferably with a lip for pouring
A thermometer is useful, but not essential
A metal pouring funnel will reduce the possibility of accidental spillage, but is not essential
A short length of stiff wire long enough to span the width of the cup. If wire is not available, a long nail, pencil or even a metal knitting needle will do
A small metal washer or nut for use as a weight
A suitable cup. The cup is to be used as a mould, with the intention of removing the candle when it is finished. It is important to be certain that there are no undercuts which will prevent the candle from being removed. An undercut is any obstruction or projection which will imprison the candle in the mould. For example, although it is possible to pour molten wax into a cup with a narrow top, it will be impossible to take the solid candle out unless the cup is first broken. To be absolutely sure that a cup has no undercuts, choose one which is wider at the top than at the bottom as illustrated.

Figure 33

54

To make the candle

Break the paraffin wax into small pieces, put them into the saucepan and heat gently. Add the oil soluble dye and stir the contents of the saucepan until the wax has all melted and the dye dissolved, then remove the saucepan and allow it to stand until the wax has cooled a little.

Tie one end of the wick to the centre of the wire, and fix the weight to the other end of the wick (*figure 34a*). Then rest the wire across the rim of the cup so that the wick is suspended in the middle as illustrated (*figure 34b*).

Now pour the wax into the cup. If a thermometer is being used, the best temperature for pouring the wax is about 82°C (180°F). If there is no thermometer, look at the saucepan to see if the wax is smoking. If it is then the wax is too hot, and should be left to cool for a little longer.

When the wax has become solid, it will contract away from the sides of the cup and can be removed easily by lifting the wick.

Figure 34   *a*   *b*

15 Making a striped candle
in a tin

Materials
454 g (1 lb) of candle wax
140 mm (5 to 6 in.) of candle wick (allow two inches more than the depth of the tin)
$\frac{1}{4}$ of a level teaspoonful of blue oil soluble dye
$\frac{1}{4}$ of a level teaspoonful of yellow oil soluble dye

Equipment
Two small saucepans, each with a lip for pouring
A thermometer is useful but not essential
A metal funnel will reduce the possibility of spillage, but is not essential
A metal rod or wire, long enough to span the top of the tin. A nail or even a pencil will do
A small nut or metal washer to serve as a weight
A suitable tin. Tins are available in a wide variety of sizes and shapes. The technique remains the same whatever shape is selected.

To make the candle
Choose the tin and clean it carefully. There must be no trace of the original contents left to mar the surface of the candle. With a tin opener, cut off the top rim—this is to prevent it acting as an undercut and imprisoning the finished candle in the mould.

Take the paraffin wax, break it into small pieces—the smaller the pieces the less time is required for melting— and put half of it in each saucepan. Add the blue dye to one saucepan, and the yellow dye to the other.

Figure 35

57

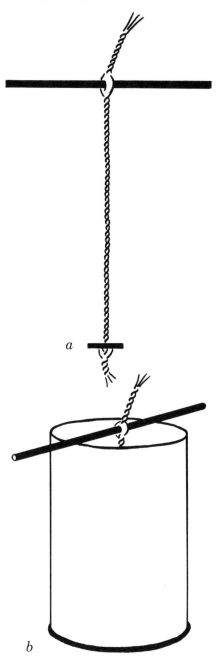

Place the saucepan containing the colour which is to be used first on the cooker and heat gently, stirring the wax until all the dye has been dissolved in the melted wax. Then remove the saucepan from the cooker, and allow the wax to cool slightly.

Take the wick, and tie the metal weight to one end, and the metal rod or wire to the other end so that the wick and wire make the shape of a 'T' (*figure 36a*). Then place the metal rod across the open top of the tin so that the wick is suspended in the middle of the tin with the weight just touching the bottom (*figure 36b*).

Now pour in the first colour to a depth of about 25 mm (1 in.); the best temperature at which to pour the wax is about 82°C (180°F), but in the absence of a thermometer, as long as there is no trace of smoke rising from the wax the temperature is acceptable. It is important not to add each additional layer too soon as if the previous layer is still liquid, the colours will blend together.

The third and fourth stripes should then be poured in turn, allowing each one to solidify before pouring the next one.

When the wax has completely set, it will contract and shrink away from the sides of the tin, making it very easy to withdraw the candle by lifting the wick.

After the candle has been removed from the tin, all that remains to be done is to cut off the surplus wick leaving about 12 mm (½ in.) projecting from the candle.

Under no circumstances should wax be melted in a tin, as they have soldered seams which could leak. Always melt wax in a seamless container such as a saucepan.

a

b   *Figure 36*

16 Making a mosaic candle in a glass tumbler

Materials
454 g (1 lb) of candle wax
127 mm to 203 mm (6 to 8 in.) of candle wick (allow two inches more than the depth of the tumbler)
$\frac{1}{4}$ of a level teaspoonful of red oil soluble dye
$\frac{1}{4}$ of a level teaspoonful of yellow oil soluble dye

Equipment
A small saucepan in which to melt the wax. It is more convenient if the saucepan has a lip which can be used for pouring
A thermometer is not essential, but is very useful
A piece of rigid wire, long enough to span the top of the glass tumbler; a pencil or metal knitting needle will do
A small metal nut or washer for use as a weight
A shallow dish or plate in which to make the wax mosaic pieces (tesserae)
A glass tumbler for use as a mould. When selecting the tumbler, make certain that there are no undercuts which will prevent the finished candle from being removed from the mould. An undercut is any projection which will obstruct the candle and lock it into the mould. For example, although it is possible to pour melted wax into a glass with a narrow rim, it will not be possible to withdraw the candle after the wax has solidified, unless the glass is broken first. Choose a tumbler with straight sides, which is wider at the top than at the bottom as illustrated.

Figure 37

59

To make the candle
Take half the paraffin wax, break it into small pieces and place in the saucepan. Add the red dye to the wax and heat the saucepan gently. When the wax has melted and the dye dissolved, pour it into the shallow dish or plate, and allow the wax to set (*figure 38*).

Figure 38

Tie one end of the wick to the middle of the wire, and fix the weight on the other end of the wick as illustrated (*figure 39*).

Warm the glass in an oven or over a gas jet. Do not submerge it in hot water as water and hot wax are incompatible and will splutter and spit unpleasantly.

Rest the wire rod across the top of the glass so that the wick is suspended in the middle of the glass with the weight just touching the bottom.

Take the solid red wax from the dish or plate in which it was poured, and break it into small pieces about 12 mm ($\frac{1}{2}$ in.) square. Place these small pieces of solid wax in the glass around the wick, filling the glass to the top. Be careful not to disturb the wick—it must remain in the centre of the candle.

Now melt the remainder of the original wax, add the yellow dye and when it has all melted and the dye dissolved, allow it to cool to about 71°C (160°F). If this wax is poured when it is too hot, it will melt all the mosaic pieces, but if it is poured at a lower temperature, it will bind them together in such a way that they will be exposed wherever they are in contact with the surface of the glass.

When the wax has set the mosaic candle can be removed from the mould, and the wick trimmed down to leave about 12 mm ($\frac{1}{2}$ in.) exposed.

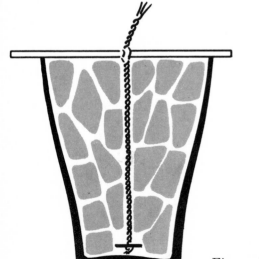

Figure 39

17 Making a two tone multiwick candle in a tin

Materials
454 g (1 lb) of candle wax
254 mm (10 in.) of candle wick
$\frac{1}{4}$ of a level teaspoonful of orange oil soluble dye
$\frac{1}{4}$ of a level teaspoonful of mauve oil soluble dye

Equipment
A small saucepan in which to melt the wax, preferably with a pouring lip
A thermometer is not essential but is very useful
A metal pouring funnel will reduce the possibility of accidental spillage
A wooden rod or a stiff wire, long enough to span the top of the tin
Two small metal washers to serve as weights

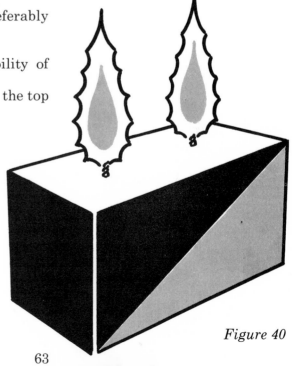

Figure 40

A suitable tin. As this candle is intended to have two wicks, a luncheon meat tin is most suitable because there is sufficient space for the wicks to be placed side by side.

To make the candle

The first job is to make sure that the tin is absolutely clean, if any of the original contents are left in the tin, they will be embedded in the surface of the candle and will spoil its appearance. The tin should be thoroughly washed and dried.

Using a tin opener or tin snips, cut off the top rim of the tin to prevent it from obstructing the removal of the finished candle.

Take half of the paraffin wax, and melt it in the saucepan, adding the orange oil soluble dye and stirring until all the dye has dissolved. When all the wax has melted, remove the saucepan from the heat and allow the wax to cool slightly.

Take the candle wick and cut it in half, tie one end of each short wick to the metal or wooden rod, and tie a metal washer to the other end of each wick (*figure 41*). The wicks should be spaced at least 50 mm (2 in.) apart. If they are too near then the close proximity of the flames when the candle is lit will cause it to burn unevenly.

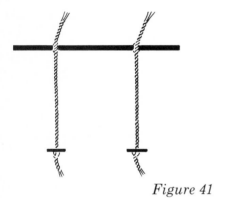

Figure 41

The wicks can now be suspended in the mould by placing the rod across the top of the tin lengthways as illustrated (*figure 42*).

Now take the saucepan and pour a little wax into the tin. At this stage a layer 3 mm ($\frac{1}{8}$ in.) deep will be enough (*figure 43a*). This initial layer is intended to fix the bottom of the wicks in position so that they cannot swing off centre when the tin is tilted to achieve the oblique two tone effect. When the first small layer of wax has set, tilt the tin as illustrated (*figure 45b*) and pour the rest of the wax from the saucepan to complete the orange layer.

While the orange wax is setting, melt down the rest of the wax, add the mauve oil soluble dye and allow the wax to cool after it has all melted and the dye dissolved.

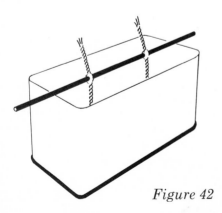

Figure 42

When the orange wax has set in the tin, return it to the vertical position (*figure 43c*) and fill the remaining space in the tin with the mauve wax.

When all the wax in the tin has set hard, it will contract away from the sides of the tin, and the solid candle can easily be removed by lifting the metal rod onto which the wicks are tied.

All that now remains to be done is to untie the wicks and trim them with a pair of scissors so that only about 12 mm ($\frac{1}{2}$ in.) of each wick is left projecting from the top of the candle.

Although there is a great temptation to use old discarded tins to melt the wax, it is important that tins should only be used as moulds as they have soldered seams which could leak if exposed to direct heat. Always melt wax in seamless containers such as a saucepan.

Figure 43

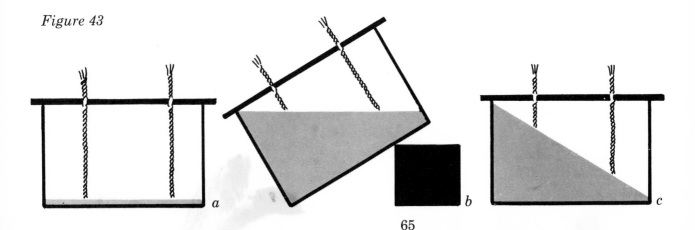

18 Making a candle with slanting stripes in a bottle

Materials
907 g (2 lb) of candle wax
25 mm (10 to 12 in.) of candle wick
$\frac{1}{2}$ level teaspoonful of orange oil soluble dye
$\frac{1}{2}$ level teaspoonful of red oil soluble dye

Equipment
Two small saucepans, each with a lip for pouring
A thermometer is useful, but not essential
A metal funnel is essential, as the neck of the bottle is too narrow to permit filling without the aid of a funnel
A metal rod or wire long enough to span the neck of the bottle
A small metal washer or nut for use as a weight
A suitable bottle. It is possible to obtain bottles in many shapes and sizes, but remember that it will be necessary to break the bottle in order to remove the finished candle, so do not choose an exotic hand blown bottle
A plastic bag large enough to contain the bottle
A hammer

Figure 44

To make the candle

Take the paraffin wax, break it into small pieces and put half of it in each saucepan. Add the red dye to one saucepan and the orange dye to the other.

Place the saucepan containing the colour to be used first on the cooker, heat gently and stir until all the dye has dissolved in the melted wax. When all the wax has melted, remove the saucepan from the cooker, and allow the wax to cool slightly.

Take the wick and tie one end to the middle of the metal rod, then tie the other end to the metal weight as illustrated (*figure 32a*).

Warm the bottle in an oven, or over a gas jet. Do not warm it with hot water, as water and hot wax are incompatible and they will splutter and spit if mixed together.

Then suspend the wick in the bottle by placing the metal rod across the top: the metal weight should just touch the bottom of the bottle.

Insert the funnel into the neck of the bottle, and pour in the first layer of wax, to a depth of about 18 mm ($\frac{3}{4}$ in.) (*figure 45a*).

It is very important to allow this first layer to become solid because it will be necessary to tilt the bottle in order to achieve slanting stripes, and the bottom layer of wax is used to maintain the position of the wick. When the bottom layer of wax has set, the bottle can be tilted and the rest of the first colour stripe added (*figure 45b*).

Heat the saucepan containing the wax of the other colour. When it has all melted, allow it to cool. The best temperature at which to pour is in the region of 82°C (180°F), but before pouring it into the bottle, make sure that the previous layer has hardened at least to the extent that a hard skin has formed on the surface. If the next colour is added before the previous layer has hardened, the two colours will blend together.

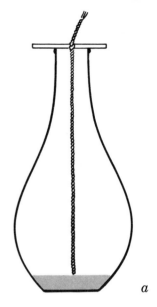

a

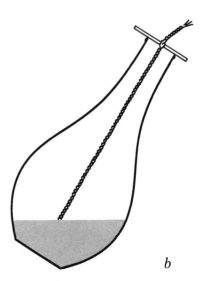

Figure 45

b

67

When the second stripe has hardened the third layer of wax can be poured in, and after that has solidified the fourth stripe can be added. The bottle should then be straightened up into a vertical position and topped up to form the fifth stripe.

When all the stripes have been poured, the candle should be left for at least five hours before attempting to remove it from the bottle.

There is only one safe way to remove a candle from a bottle, and that is to place the bottle in a large plastic bag, shatter the bottle with a hammer and then withdraw only the candle leaving the broken glass untouched in the bag.

After removing the candle from the bag, all that remains to be done is to cut the wick down so that only 12 mm ($\frac{1}{2}$ in.) is left projecting from the top of the candle.

19 Making a spherical candle in a plaster mould

Materials for the mould
A smooth rubber ball about 75 mm (3 in.) in diameter
454 g (1 lb) of plasticine
3 kg (6 lb) of plaster of paris
1 small tin of polyurethane paint
1 small tube of glue
1 sheet of fine grain cardboard
A small jar of petroleum jelly or vaseline

Materials for the candle
454 g (1 lb) of candle wax
152 mm (6 in.) of candle wick
1 metal or wooden rod about 152 mm (6 in.) long

To make the mould
Measure the diameter of the rubber ball, and cut a hole of the same size in the sheet of cardboard as illustrated (*figure 47*).

Cut out the corners of the cardboard as shown (*figure 48*) and fold the sides to form a shallow box.

Glue the corners; paper clips or pins can be used to hold the corners in position while the glue is setting.

Place the ball in the hole so that the cardboard is level with the middle of the ball (*figure 49*). If the ball is examined closely it is generally possible to see a faint line around the middle indicating where the two halves of the original manufacturer's mould met. This is known as the

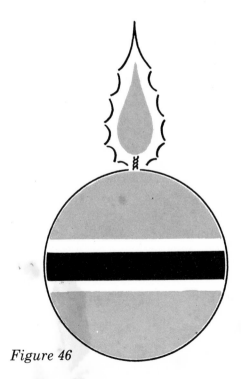

Figure 46

flash line and is useful as a guide for positioning the ball in the cardboard. It is extremely important that the ball is inserted exactly to its centre line, as if it is even slightly off centre it may create an undercut (obstruction) which could make it difficult to remove the candle from the finished mould.

When the ball is in position it should be firmly wedged in place with the plasticine as illustrated.

Make a ball of plasticine about 12 mm ($\frac{1}{2}$ in.) in diameter, cut it in half and place the halves in diagonally opposite corners of the box.

Now take more plasticine and roll it into a cylinder about 50 mm (2 in.) in diameter and cut it in half lengthways. Take one half and tailor it to fit between the ball and the side of the box.

Now apply a thin layer of petroleum jelly or vaseline to the inside of the box and everything in it.

All that now remains to be done in order to finish the first half of the plaster mould is to support the box so that it is horizontal and no weight is resting on the rubber ball, and then the plaster can be poured (*figure 50*).

The best technique for mixing plaster is to put the water into a polythene bowl and sprinkle the plaster into the

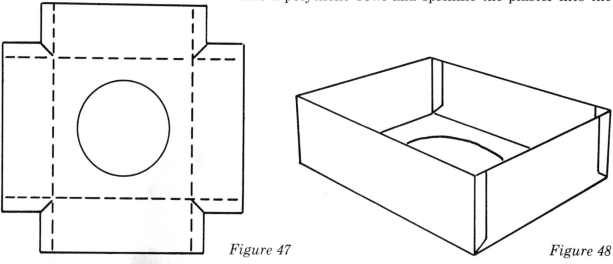

Figure 47

Figure 48

water stirring until it has the consistency of thick cream. The proportion of plaster to water should be in the region of three pounds of plaster to one pint of water.

When the plaster is ready, pour it into one corner of the box so that it rises around the ball excluding all air from the mould surface.

Allow the plaster to set for half an hour and then remove the plasticine and the cardboard leaving the ball half embedded in the plaster.

Construct a cardboard wall around the plaster block and add the second half of the plasticine cylinder, tailoring it to fit as before.

Scoop out the hemispheres of plasticine from the corners of the plaster block and coat the whole of the inside of the box and plaster with vaseline (*figure 51*).

Now mix up the rest of the plaster and pour it into the corner of the box allowing it to rise up over the exposed half ball. When the plaster has set the cardboard can be removed, the mould opened and the ball and plasticine pulled out of each half.

With a sharp knife, cut a channel for the wick as illustrated or alternatively the mould can be closed and a

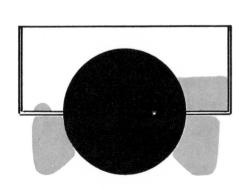

Figure 49

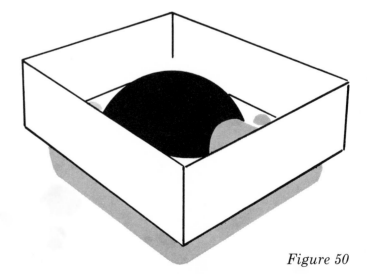

Figure 50

71

hole 2 mm ($\frac{3}{32}$ in.) drilled exactly between the two halves of the mould so that each half contains half of the wick channel.

The candle mould should then be allowed to dry out for a few days and then painted with two coats of clear polyurethane paint. The mould is now ready for use (*figure 52*).

To make the candle

Melt the wax in the saucepan. Break the wax into small pieces, place it in the saucepan and heat gently. Add the oil soluble dye and stir until it has all dissolved. When all the wax has melted remove the saucepan from the heat source and allow the wax to cool.

Tie one end of the wick to the centre of the metal rod, place the rod across the top of the open mould, run the wick down through the wick channel, and close the mould, fixing it with strong elastic bands or string (*figure 53*).

Pull the wick taut and seal it with a piece of plasticine underneath the wick channel.

When the temperature of the wax in the saucepan has fallen to about 79°C (175°F) pour it into the mould through the tea strainer and pouring funnel. As this is a two piece mould it is important not to pour the wax at too high a temperature as it could then leak through the joint between the two halves of the mould.

As the wax cools, it contracts and it will be necessary to top the mould up with hot wax after an hour or so.

When the wax has completely set, it will shrink away from the sides of the mould, and the candle can easily be removed after the mould has been opened.

All that now remains to be done is to trim the base of the candle with a sharp knife and to cut the wick so that about a 12 mm ($\frac{1}{2}$ in.) is left projecting from the top of the candle.

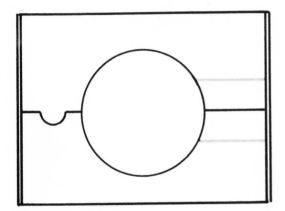

Figure 51

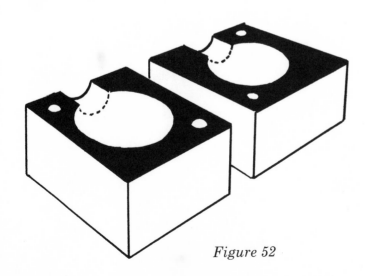

Figure 52

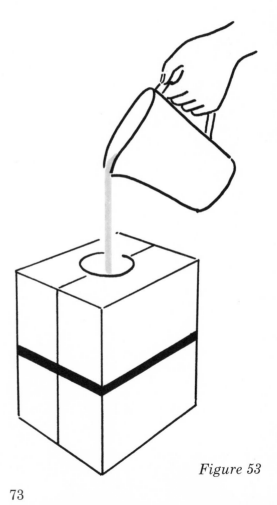

Figure 53

20 Making a conical candle in a cardboard mould

Figure 54

Materials for the mould
1 sheet of fine grain cardboard such as Bristolboard
1 roll of adhesive paper tape 25 mm (1 in.) wide
1 small tin of polyurethane paint
1 small tube of any contact glue

Materials for the candle
565 g (1¼ lb) of candle wax
290 mm (11 in.) of candle wick
½ a level teaspoonful of oil soluble dye

Equipment
A small saucepan with a pouring lip
A thermometer
A metal pouring funnel
A metal or wooden rod long enough to span the widest point of the cone
A ball of plasticine about 25 mm (1 in.) in diameter
A small cardboard box

To make the mould
Transfer the pattern to the cardboard: each square of the graph represents 10 mm (⅜ in.) but can be scaled up or down as required (*figure 55*).

After the pattern has been drawn and cut out, bend the cardboard into the shape of a cone leaving a hole about 2 mm (1/16 in.) in diameter at the pointed end. Mark where

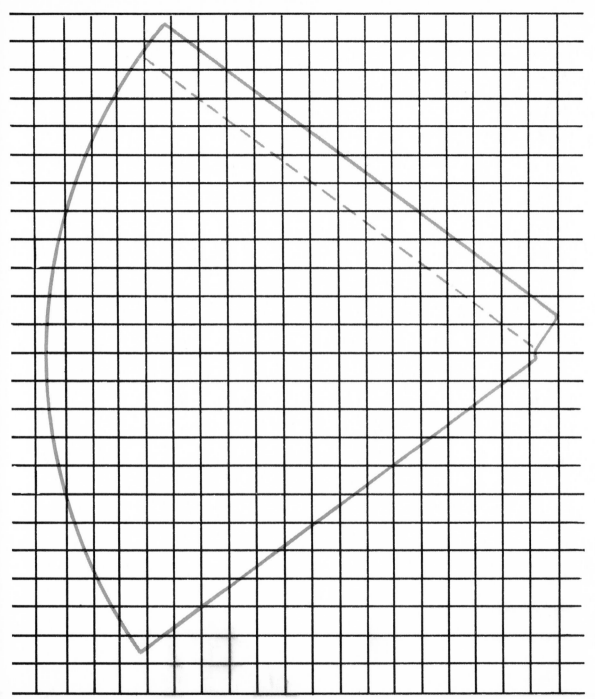

Figure 55

the overlap ends by running a pencil down the outside seam, open the cone and apply the glue to the area of the overlap. Bend the cardboard around into a cone again and keep it in position with a paper clip while the glue sets.

The outside seam should then be completely sealed with adhesive paper tape as illustrated (*figure 56a*) and the paper clip removed.

When the glue has been allowed to set paint the inside of the cone with two coats of polyurethane paint. When the paint is completely dry, the mould is complete and ready for use.

To make the candle
Insert one end of the wick into the hole in the pointed end of the cone, push the wick through until it reaches the wide end, and tie it to the centre of the metal rod as illustrated. The plasticine should then be used to seal the pointed end of the cone and retain the other end of the wick (*figure 56b*).

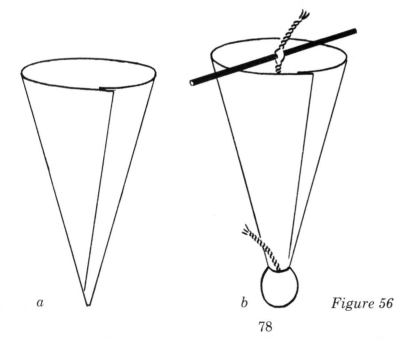

a   *b*   *Figure 56*

Now take the cardboard box and cut a hole about 65 mm (2½ in.) in diameter in the top. Then drop the cone, pointed end first into the hole. The mould is now standing upright and is ready to receive the molten wax (*figure 56c*).

Melt the candle wax in a saucepan, add the dye and when the wax has melted and the dye dissolved, remove the saucepan from the heat and allow it to cool to about 82°C (180°F). Do not pour the wax too hot or it will melt the plasticine and drain out of the mould making an unpleasant mess.

Using the funnel, pour the wax through the metal tea strainer until the mould is filled. Do not allow the wax to cascade into the mould as this will trap air bubbles against the mould walls and spoil the surface of the finished candle. Any dirt or fluff contained in the wax will be filtered out by the tea strainer.

When the wax has completely set, it will contract away from the sides of the mould allowing the candle to be removed easily.

Once the candle is out of the mould, all that remains to be done is to trim the bottom of the candle with a sharp knife, if necessary, and cut down the wick so that only 12 mm (½ in.) is left projecting from the top of the candle.

As the wax cools, it will contract and it may be necessary to top it up with hot wax after two hours or so. It is also advisable to poke a pencil or knitting needle into the wax beside the wick to release the vacuum.

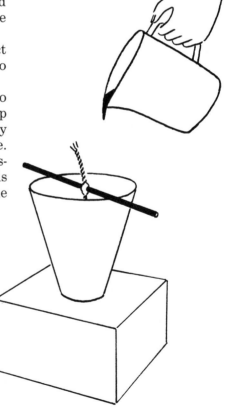

c

79

21 Making a candle in a metal jelly mould

Jelly moulds are available in many shapes and sizes, and can be used to make exciting and interesting candles which are ideal gifts for children.

For the purposes of this chapter, a jelly mould in the shape of a rabbit was chosen (*figure 57*), because its long low shape provided an opportunity to incorporate multiple wicks so that the candle could be used as an original centre piece for a birthday party. Up to six wicks could be fitted according to the size of the jelly mould.

When making a candle in a jelly mould, it is important to use only metal jelly moulds, as plastic ones may collapse when filled with hot wax. This is because wax can be heated to a much higher temperature than hot jelly which contains water and evaporates into steam at 100°C (212°F).

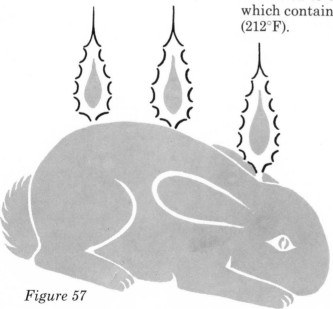

Figure 57

There are two ways of fitting the wicks to a jelly mould candle. The best way is to cast the wax into the mould and then fit the wicks after the wax has set and been removed from the mould. This is done by drilling holes in the solid wax, and simply threading the wicks through the holes (*figure 58*). The wicks should first be dipped in hot wax and allowed to cool. The second way to fit the wicks involves drilling holes in the bottom of the jelly mould and applying the wicks as illustrated (*figure 59*), but as this method ruins the mould for jelly making it is not recommended.

A hard candle wax is advisable for use with jelly moulds, and if a translucent wax is used, coloured yellow, orange or red, the whole rabbit will light up when the candle is lit.

Equipment
A saucepan with a pouring lip
A metal jelly mould
A confectionery thermometer
A 3 mm ($\frac{1}{8}$ in.) drill for drilling holes in the candle to take the wicks

Figure 58

Materials
907 g (2 lb) of translucent candle wax—more if the jelly mould is very large
Candle wick—allow 127 mm (5 in.) for each wick to be used
$\frac{1}{4}$ level teaspoonful of oil soluble dye

To make the candle
Break the candle wax into small pieces, place it in the saucepan and heat gently. Stir in the oil soluble dye, and when all the wax has melted, remove the saucepan from the heat source and allow it to cool slightly. Dip the candle wicks into the hot wax, pull them straight and place them on a flat surface to cool. When the temperature of the wax has cooled to about 82°C (180°F), pour the wax into the jelly mould, do not allow it to cascade or air bubbles will be trapped against the sides of the mould, spoiling the surface of the finished candle.

When the wax has set, remove the candle from the mould. It should drop out quite easily. Drill the required number of holes through the wax and insert the wicks, allowing about 12 mm ($\frac{1}{2}$ in.) of wick to project from the top of the candle.

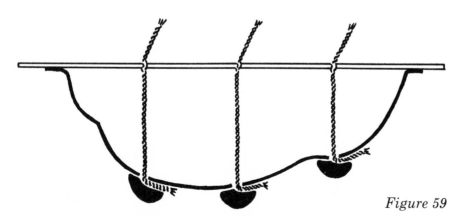

Figure 59

22 Making figurine candles

Figure 60

There are people skilled enough to model an original candle shape in clay, and to make from it a plaster of paris candle mould. But for those of us who lack this skill, or the time to acquire it, there is a short cut. Many articles are made from moulds similar to those used for candles, so it is quite possible for the ambitious domestic candle maker to make a plaster candle mould using a ready made article to give the shape. The variety of suitable articles is enormous, for toys, soap figures and glazed pottery figurines can all be used to make candle moulds with excellent results. As the technique of mould making is exactly the same as described in Chapter 12 there is no need to repeat the details of making a plaster mould. Let us instead concentrate on what sort of shape to choose and what to avoid.

When choosing a figure for this purpose it is important to be certain that it is mouldable, in other words there must be no undercuts or obstructions which could prevent the removal of the solid candle from the mould. As it is often difficult to appreciate the presence of undercuts, the problem can be made much easier by consciously choosing an article known to have been moulded already. All moulded and cast articles show a faint line where the separate parts of the original mould joined together. This line is called the *flash line*, and if the domestic candle maker divides the plaster mould at the same place there should be no trouble with withdrawal or undercuts.

On examining the flash line of the chosen article, if it

Figure 61

is not straight (sometimes it follows the centre of an arm or a leg) the base of the first half of the plaster mould will have to be built up with clay instead of the cardboard cut out described in Chapter 12.

To demonstrate the availability of toys suitable for this purpose, I hunted through my young son's toy box. The first suitable toy which came to hand was a small plastic bear which had originally been the top of a rattle; the second one was the remains of a skittle in the form of a soldier standing to attention; the third one was an enormous clown weighted at the bottom so that it could not fall over; and the fourth one was a plastic dog which was intended as a toothbrush holder. There was obviously no shortage of toys suitable for making plaster candle moulds.

Soap is moulded in a wide variety of decorative figures —one only has to look in the windows of a large chemist's shop to see just how large the choice is. Soap figures are particularly suitable for the purposes of mould making as they are made in moulds very similar to those used for candles, and often the flash line is very clearly marked.

For those interested in making a candle mould from a pottery or porcelain figurine, the same degree of mouldability is required, and if possible a flash line should be used as a guide. It is important to choose a simple compact figurine, as the more complicated ones are either hand modelled or assembled from several different components. In both cases mould making becomes very difficult if not impossible.

Figurine candles can be painted if required, but a *shellac*-based paint should be used.

23 Decorative effects

Candles can be decorated in a wide variety of ways. They can be striped, made to look like mosaic, carved, aerated, painted and marbled.

'In mould' stripes
Candles made by the casting process can be striped by the 'in mould' technique. This technique consists of filling the mould with separate layers of wax, each layer being of a different colour. When making striped candles in this way each layer must be allowed to solidify before adding the next colour, as if the previous layer of wax is still in liquid form the different colours will just blend together into one.

Slanting stripes can be made by tilting the mould. As it is important for the wick to remain in a central position, it must be securely fixed at both ends of the mould so that it cannot swing or sag out of position. This is no problem if the mould is of the purpose made type with the wick running through a hole in the bottom, but if the wick is just hanging with a weight on the end, a small amount of wax must be poured in first and allowed to set before the mould is tilted so that the slanted stripes can be poured.

Dipped stripes
Colour stripes can be applied to a candle by the dipping process. This is an ideal way to decorate ordinary domestic candles. The process consists of dipping one end of a candle into a saucepan of molten wax, removing it,

85

allowing the coating to cool and then reversing the candle and dipping the other end of it into molten wax of a different colour.

A candle wax blend should be used for this dipping process. It should consist of semi refined paraffin wax with a melting point of 52°C to 54°C (125°F to 130°F) blended with 30% stearic acid. The dipping temperature should be in the region of 49°C (120°F), but it will depend largely on the type of wax used.

Dipped multiple stripes
If multiple stripes are required, the basic process remains the same but the lightest colour should be dipped first and then partially overdipped with the darker colours. For example if red, orange and yellow stripes are required, first dip the candle into yellow wax, then overdip two thirds of it in orange and finally overdip half of the orange coating with red wax.

If even more stripes are required, the number of colour stripes can almost be doubled by making the stripes narrower, and reversing the candle.

Random mosaic
A mosaic effect can be obtained by filling the mould with chips of solid coloured wax, and then topping up the mould with molten wax to bind all the coloured chips together. The molten wax should be relatively low in temperature, about 71°C (160°F), as if it is too hot it will melt the coloured chips. Care must be taken not to dislodge the wick from its central position, as the candle will burn badly if the wick is not in the middle when the candle has set.

Marbling
A marble like effect can be achieved if a teaspoonful of oil is added to the molten wax. The oil should be added immediately after the mould has been filled, and will follow the convection currents through the molten wax. If the oil is slightly tinted with oil soluble dye, the effect

will be much bolder. The general effect of marble can be further improved by using a blend consisting of translucent fully refined paraffin wax with a melting point of 60°C to 63°C (140°F to 145°F) and 3% of micro crystalline wax.

Aerated wax
Air bubbles can be introduced into wax by beating it as it cools. Wax which has been aerated in this way can be used for casting, but if stripes are required a low temperature paraffin wax must be used otherwise the separate layers of wax will not bond together.

Painting
Wax can be painted. The best paint for the purpose is a natural shellac based paint. Although all candles can be painted, it is better to limit painting to large diameter candles, as if a thin candle is painted, the relatively high proportion of paint to wax may adversely affect the burning qualities of the candle.

Applied decoration
Some people like to apply surface decoration in the form of paper cutouts. Such decoration can be applied with the aid of gum arabic.

Ice mosaic
An interesting effect can be obtained by filling the mould with pieces of ice instead of pieces of solid wax. When the finished candle is removed from the mould and the ice has melted, the resulting candle is honeycombed with cavities. It is essential to dip the wick in molten wax before filling the mould with ice. If this is not done the wick may absorb water from the ice which could cause the candle flame to splutter and spit when it is eventually lit.

Metal foil infill
Crumpled pieces of aluminium foil can be placed in the

mould after it has been filled and, provided the candle is made from translucent wax, they give a very intriguing visual effect.

Moulded surface patterns and textures
Softened candle wax can be modelled by hand and literally stuck on to the surface of the candle to form a rich texture in bas relief. As candle wax requires more than hand heat to melt it a container of hot water should be at hand in which to soften the wax. The temperature of the water should not exceed 41°C (105°F) or the wax will tend to melt and not soften.

After modelling the decoration in wax it can be stuck on to the body of the candle in one of two ways. It can be glued with the oil of a little hot glutinous wax such as beeswax, or it can be welded on with the aid of a heated metal tool—any piece of metal will do, for example a pair of scissors, or a screwdriver or knife blade. The metal tool is heated on a conveniently situated lighted candle, and then firmly but gently pressed into the edge of the wax decoration so that both it and the base candle melt and fuse.

The welding process can be developed into a technique for decorating candles in its own right. A thin roll of wax welded to a candle will display indentation whenever the hot tool is used. These indentations if repeated frequently, form a texture which can be developed into an overall pattern. The pattern is emphasized by the small layer of soot deposited by the hot tool. The tool becomes sooty through being heated over a flame. This shading of indentation can be exaggerated by rubbing in powdered graphite or carbon. Any excess can be removed with a cloth dipped in turpentine leaving only the indentations coloured.

Pressed decoration
Decorative panels can be made by pressing wax into shallow moulds made from plaster or lino. In both cases the technique is the same; the pattern is carved into a

flat block of plaster or lino, and then a flattened sheet of wax warmed in hot water 41°C (105°F) and pressed firmly onto the mould until it assumes the bas relief pattern on the reverse side. The decorative panels can then be trimmed to shape and glued on to the mould with a dab of hot beeswax. Decoration can be added as small pieces or as complete bands encircling the whole candle.

Cut out decoration
Flat sheets of coloured wax about a sixteenth of an inch thick can be cast into shallow baking dishes (a silicone release agent should be used for ease of removal) and then cut up with scissors and glued onto the candle shaft with a touch of hot beeswax. The wax used should be of the softer variety so that it is malleable and should have a melting point in the region of 52°C to 54°C (125°F to 130°F).

Cast decoration
Decorative panels can be cast into shallow sheets by using shallow plaster of paris moulds. Cast the plaster into a shallow mould of the type illustrated, and then carve the pattern into the smooth side which was cast against the glass. Allow the plaster to dry for several days and then paint it with clear polyurethane paint.

When the plaster mould is completely finished put it back into the original wooden frame which should also be finished in polyurethane paint, and then apply the silicone release agent. The mould is then ready to receive the hot paraffin wax. A soft grade of paraffin wax should be used, with a melting point in the region of 52°C (125°F). If the wax is too brittle to be applied to the candle, it can be softened by adding 30% of beeswax to it. It will be necessary to warm the decorative panel in order to tailor it to fit the candle. This can be done in an oven, though hot water is more suitable, but it should not be over 41°C (105°F) in temperature or the wax will tend to melt rather than soften.

International suppliers of candlemaking materials

This list is not exhaustive. There are many other suppliers, and their addresses can be obtained from the classified trade directories of the countries concerned.

GREAT BRITAIN
Candle making materials are stocked by very few handicraft shops in Great Britain, but all materials are available by post from:

Candle Kit
129 Rosendale Road
West Dulwich
London, SE 21 8HE
who will send a price list on receipt of a stamped and addressed envelope.

Candlemaker's Supplies
4 Beaconsfield Terrace Road
(off Blythe Road)
London, W 14

Wincan
369 Church Lane
Kingsbury
London, NW 9

Legendcraft
21 Coombe Road
Otford, Kent

Materials in large quantities are also available from the following sources:

Oil soluble dyes
Imperial Chemical Industries
(Dyestuffs Division)
Hexagon House, Manchester 9

Sandoz Products Limited
208 Acton Lane
London, NW 10

Stearine
Wynmouth Lehr and Fatoils Limited
158 City Road
London, EC 1

Croda Chemicals Limited
Universal Division
Cunard House
88 Leadenhall Street
London, EC 3

Waxes
Burmah Oil Waxes Limited
Thames Road, Crayford, Kent

Poth, Hille and Company Limited
High Street
Stratford, London, E 15

Shell Chemicals UK Limited
Carrington
Urmston, Manchester, M31 4AJ

Wicks
Hayes and Finch Limited
30/38 Vernon Street
Liverpool

Ripley Weaving Company Limited
Wellington Hills
Ripley, Derby

UNITED STATES
Candle making materials are very easy to obtain in the
United States, and are stocked by most handicraft shops
and departmental stores. For those interested in purchasing materials in large quantities, they may be obtained
from the following suppliers:

Oil soluble dyes
General Aniline and Film Corporation
140 West 51 Street
New York

Stearine
Proctor and Gamble Company
PO Box 599
Cincinnati, Ohio

Waxes
Cornelius Wax Refining Corporation
1711 Elizabeth Avenue West
Linden, New Jersey

Moore and Munger
777 Summer Street
Stamford Street
Stamford, Connecticut

Frank B. Ross Company Inc
6 Ash Street
Jersey City 4, New Jersey

Wicks
Atkins and Pearce Manufacturing Company
Pike and Pearl Street
Cincinnati, Ohio

AUSTRALIA
Few handicraft shops stock candle making materials in
Australia, but they are available from the following
sources:

Oil soluble dyes
Yorkshire Dyeware and Chemical Company
Rooney Street
Richmond, Victoria

Stearine
H. C. Sleigh Limited
160 Queen Street
Melbourne, Victoria

Marrickville Margarine Limited
74 Edinborough Road
Marrickville, New South Wales

Waxes
Houghton and Byrne (Prop) Limited
225 George Street
Sydney, New South Wales

Wicks
Gover Carr (Prop) Limited
Tangarra Street
Croydon Park
Sydney, New South Wales

Felt and Textiles of Australia Limited
8 Nickolson Street
East Melbourne, Victoria

NEW ZEALAND
Candle making materials are not usually stocked by handicraft shops in New Zealand, but materials may be available from the following sources:

Candle manufacturers
Zealandia Soap, Candle and Trading Company
P.O. Box 8
Belfast

Golden Glo Candles Limited
P.O. Box 34–119
Birkenhead, Auckland

Candle Craft
158 Commerce Street
Whakatane

N. R. Hayes International Sales Company Limited
PO Box 2881
Auckland

Oil soluble dyes
Imperial Chemical Industries (New Zealand) Limited
PO Box 1592
Wellington

Waxes
Shell Oil (New Zealand) Limited
PO Box 2091
Wellington

CANADA

Candle making materials are generally available in Canada from handicraft and Do-It-Yourself shops, but for those people interested in purchasing direct from the manufacturers:

Oil soluble dyes
Canadian Industries Limited
PO Box 10
Montreal 101, Quebec

Stearine
Faster Fats Division
National Sea Products Limited
Lower Water Street
Halifax, Nova Scotia

Swift Canadian Company
PO Box 505
Etobicoke, Ontario.

Waxes
International Waxes Limited
50 Salome Drive
Ajincourt, Ontario

Wicks
Hamilton Cotton Company
PO Box 397
Hamilton, Ontario

SOUTH AFRICA
Very few handicraft shops stock candle making materials
in South Africa, but they may be obtained from the
following suppliers:

Oil soluble dyes
African Explosives (Pty) Limited
40 Fox Street
Johannesburg, Transvaal

Waxes
Shell South Africa (Pty) Limited
Shell House
Green Market Street
Capetown

Wicks
Braitex (Pty) Limited
24 Marconi Street
New Era Township
Springs, Transvaal